Keep The Fire Going

Devotions For After The Mission Trip

Gabe Barrett

ISBN: 1533168997
ISBN-13: 978-1533168993

CONTENTS

DEDICATION

This book is dedicated to every person who has been a part of the M25 Mission Camp. God has done amazing things through you, and it has been an absolute pleasure to witness.

INTRODUCTION

Mission trips have gotten a lot of flack over the past few years. Books have been written and studies have been done that suggest they are a waste of time, money, and resources and that the trips don't actually do anything productive to help the world. And many churches have stopped going on mission trips because of this.

But to put it bluntly, I think that's garbage.

After leading 50+ mission trips, I've seen the power short-term mission trips have to drastically change people's lives. I've seen students and adults alike do incredible things to love and serve others. I've seen darkness lit up. I've seen people give away the shoes off of their own feet. I've seen homeless men find stable housing. I've seen the hungry fed. I've seen the out-of-work find jobs. I've seen orphans taken into families. I've seen people go back home and live completely different lives. And all of it was helped along by short-term missions.

I'm a firm believer in what mission trips have to offer the world.

However, the biggest problem with mission trips is what happens when people get home.

Usually, nothing happens when people get home.

The trip was great. The people were awesome. God moved in some really cool ways. But now it's back to reality.

This happens all the time.

But missions should be an extension of following Jesus. They're just what Christ-followers do. It's normal life. People who know Jesus don't go on mission trips. Their lives are mission trips.

When you follow Jesus, mission work isn't something extra that you do, it's just part of your daily routine. It's no different than brushing your teeth or putting clothes on.

You wouldn't walk out of your house without clothes on; why would you walk by a person in need without helping?

Was your trip just a fun experience? Did it just check a box? Did it just give you a high? Or did you experience God in such a way that it lit a fire in you to go and live differently?

And I have to ask, what's the point of going on a mission trip if you're not going to let it change you?

But I also don't want you to fall into the trap of simply chasing the next spiritual high. I've been there. And if you get on that path, you'll chase the high for the rest of your life, and nothing will ever be good enough. Trust me.

When we chase after Jesus, serving is just part of it. When we chase after serving, it's often more about us than Jesus. It's really that simple.

If you just wrapped up a trip, you're probably feeling that spiritual high right now. And please know that there's nothing wrong with that. It's normal to feel this way. The problems arise when we start loving that feeling more than Jesus and when we start doing things to get the feeling but are actually harmful to others.

But please, by all means, enjoy the high. Just know that it's going to fade. As you get back into normal life and the normal grind of things, your normal daily problems and obstacles will return, and it'll be easy to go back to living the exact same life you lived before your trip.

And it's going to take a conscious effort to not allow that to happen.

I wrote this devotional to help with that.

It'll both encourage and challenge you. And hopefully, it'll keep you moving forward.

The best part about mission trips is the power they have to change us. They open our eyes to the problems and pain of others. They show us new cultures and ways to look at things. They give us opportunities to see what God is doing in the world and be a part of it.

But your trip was useless if you don't allow it to make you different.

Please realize that God didn't create you to get work done. He created work to get you done.

You didn't go on a mission trip because God was overwhelmed and couldn't make it out to that part of the world. You went on a mission trip because God graciously allows us to take part in what He's doing in the world that He so loves.

So, now it's time to go see what God is doing in your hometown. And it's time to be a part of it.

Don't go back to ordinary life.

Keep the fire going.

1

THE MOST IMPORTANT DAY

This is the day the Lord has made; let us rejoice and be glad in it.

-Psalm 118:24

When I lived in Los Angeles, I went to a church that did a good bit of work on Skid Row. If you're not familiar with Skid Row, it's one of the toughest areas in the country. It's filled with brokenness, drug abuse, homelessness, and depression.

The first time I ever went with members of the church to serve there, we were passing out blankets and rain coats and inviting people to a big meal and worship service that was happening that night.

It was the first time I had ever really sat down to talk with people who lived on the street. It was eye opening.

As we walked around the area, I kept noticing small, metal pipes that ran along the tops of many of the buildings. They obviously served a purpose, but they looked out of place.

I asked the guy leading our group what the pipes were for.

He said they were part of a sprinkler system.

Oh, ok. That made sense I thought.

But then he said, "But the sprinklers aren't for the buildings. The landowners had them installed when people started sleeping on the sidewalks. They turn the water on to spray the people to make them move."

Wow.

People. Human beings were in a dire situation, and the people who had the means to help decided the best solution was to spray them with water so they'd go be somebody else's problem.

Again, wow.

How typical of the world's answers to difficult circumstances.

As the guy told me about the sprinklers, I got really angry on the inside. I knew I didn't have all the answers; heck, I didn't have any answers. But I knew spraying folks with water and literally washing them into the gutter wasn't the way to treat people.

Looking back, that one-day mission trip was a giant turning point in my life. It was the day I decided I had to be part of something that helped and loved people and pulled them out of the ditch. I couldn't sit on the sidelines as the world tried to throw people away.

It was a very important day in my life.

But the most important day of that experience was the next day.

Back at home, there weren't sprinklers around the tops of buildings. There weren't people sleeping on the side of the road. There weren't any of the issues I had witnessed the day before.

And it would have been incredibly easy to just think of what happened a day ago as simply a cool experience.

But a fire had been lit inside of me. I had seen Jesus in the gutter, and I had experienced God move in ways I had never experienced before.

So, now I had to make sure the fire kept going. I couldn't let the monotony of everyday life put that fire out.

"This is the day the Lord has made" has become a Christian cliché. We've cheapened its meaning to the point where it doesn't hit us like it should.

But I want you to think about that verse in the context of the day after your mission trip. God created the day after your missional experience to see what your response would be. It's a day that begs the question, "Now what?"

You saw Jesus and experienced God in some profound ways, but now what are you going to do?

I realize how hard it can be to break away from ordinary life to pursue something bigger. I get it.

So I wrote this devotional to begin on the most important day of your mission trip—**the day you go home**.

It's the most important day because it's the day you start finding out what impact the trip actually had on your life.

So, as you get back into the normal, everyday swing of things, how is your life going to be different? How are you going to take your experience forward? How are you going to keep your fire going?

What are you going to do today based on what you saw yesterday?

This is the day the Lord has made; let's rejoice, be glad, and do something with it.

2

YOUR MISSION FIELD

As Jesus was getting into the boat, the man who had been demon-possessed kept begging Him to be with Him. But He would not let him: instead, He told him, "Go back home to your own people, and report to them how much the Lord has done for you and how He has had mercy on you." So he went out and began to proclaim in the Decapolis how much Jesus had done for him, and they were all amazed.

-Mark 5:18-20

Let's set the stage for a moment. There was a crazy, depraved man with a legion of demons inside of him living amongst the tombs in a region called Decapolis. We'll call this crazy man Steve.

Jesus shows up and casts the army of demons out of Steve, but He doesn't just banish them, he transfers them into a herd of 2000 pigs. This, of course, freaks the mess out of the pigs, and they run off into the sea and drown themselves. They think, "Thanks, Steve," as they go to a watery grave.

The men in charge of the pigs freak out because ten tons of bacon just floated away, so they run off to find shoulders to cry on.

Then, a whole bunch of people from the area show up to see what all the commotion is about, and they find crazy Steve talking to Jesus and the disciples like everything is cool and like he wasn't running around a cemetery naked like seven minutes ago.

So, their bacon is gone, Steve is a normal human being, and this Jesus guy is at the center of all of it. So, now they freak out. They're terrified of Jesus, so this large crowd of people begs Him to leave the area.

But this puts Steve in a tough spot. Jesus just saved his life, and all Steve wants to do is follow and get to know Him. But Jesus gets into the boat.

Steve begs to go with Jesus. "Please!" he pleads.

But Jesus won't allow it.

Instead, Jesus tells him to "Go back home." He says to go back and tell his own people about God's mercy and about what the Lord has done for him.

I struggled with this scene for a long time. I didn't understand what the big deal was. Why couldn't Steve become the thirteenth disciple? Why couldn't he sub out with Judas? Why was Jesus so harsh and determined that he stay in that area?

But one day, I was studying Mark 7. And toward the

end of the chapter, in verse 31, it tells us that Jesus was traveling through the region of the Decapolis. That word seemed familiar, so I googled it.

And there it was. Mark chapter 5. Crazy Steve.

Decapolis is where Jesus left Steve. Decapolis is where a giant crowd of bacon loving people was afraid of Jesus and begged him to leave. Decapolis is where Steve was proclaiming the Gospel.

And as Jesus returns to the region in Mark 7 and into Mark 8, we find a very different situation. As soon as He arrives, the people bring Him a deaf man to be healed.

Then, a few days later, Jesus is surrounded by a crowd of over 4,000 people! It's one of the times when He fed a multitude with just a little bread and a few fish.

In Decapolis!

The people in this area had gone from begging Jesus to leave to hanging on His every word.

They went from being upset about their pigs to bringing Him their sick.

And I have to believe that a lot of this has to do with the testimony of a certain formerly crazed, formerly demon-possessed man who was no longer living at the cemetery.

I have to believe that Steve not going with Jesus but instead going back to his home and his people is what helped pave the way for Jesus's return to the area.

So, maybe Jesus wasn't being harsh and cold when He wouldn't let Steve go with Him. Maybe there was a bigger plan.

As your mission trip comes to an end, and you make your way back home, it's easy to wish you were still out in the mission field serving. It's common to want to continue working with the people you met. It's normal to wish you had just a little more time to do a little more good.

But it's time to go home.

It's time to go back to your own people.

It's time to go tell them about God's mercy and what He has done for you.

Please understand that you have been placed there for a reason. It was a strategic move to put you in that area and with those people.

And I assure you that God is at work just as much there as any other place in the world.

But do you see it?

Are you a part of what God is doing there?

It's your mission field. It might not be as interesting or "fulfilling" as another country or another city, but it's yours.

It's the place God has you.

And you have an incredible opportunity there.

3

ENJOY BREAKFAST

Later, by the Sea of Tiberias, Jesus again revealed Himself to the disciples. He made Himself known in this way: Simon Peter, Thomas called Didymus, Nathanael from Cana in Galilee, the sons of Zebedee, and two other disciples were together. Simon Peter told them, "I am going fishing."

"We will go with you," they said. So they went out and got into the boat, but caught nothing that night.

Early in the morning, Jesus stood on the shore, but the disciples did not recognize that it was Jesus. So He said to them, "Children, do you have any fish?"

"No," they answered.

He told them, "Cast the net on the right side of the boat, and you will find some." So they cast it there, and they were unable to haul it in because of the great number of fish.

Then the disciple whom Jesus loved said to Peter, "It is the Lord!" As soon as Simon Peter heard that it was the

Lord, he put on his outer garment (for he had removed it) and jumped into the sea. The other disciples came ashore in the boat. They dragged in the net full of fish, for they were not far from land, only about a hundred yards.

When they landed, they saw that a charcoal fire had been prepared, with fish on it, and some bread.

Jesus told them, "Bring some of the fish you have just caught." So Simon Peter went aboard and dragged the net ashore. It was full of large fish, one hundred fifty-three. And although there were so many, the net was not torn.

"Come, have breakfast," Jesus said to them. None of the disciples dared to ask Him, "Who are You?" They knew it was the Lord. Jesus came and took the bread and gave it to them, and He did the same with the fish.

-John 21:1-13

This might be my all time favorite scene in all of scripture. It's not one that gets preached on very often, but I believe it showcases God's character and love for us in an incredible way.

But to truly understand what's going on, we have to go back a little bit.

Just a matter of days prior to Jesus showing up on the shore, He had been crucified and laid in a tomb. And not long before that, Peter had denied even knowing

Jesus three times. And just a little before that, Peter had declared that even if he had to die, he would **never** disown Jesus.

So, Peter was in a pretty bad spot. He had made this adamant declaration. He claimed allegiance to Jesus even to the point of death. He made it very clear that nothing would separate him from Jesus.

Then, just hours later, not a year or even a week or two, but HOURS LATER, Peter says he doesn't even know who Jesus is. And he wasn't being questioned by a group of intimidating soldiers. He wasn't being interrogated.

He was talking to a little girl.

Peter couldn't even stand up to a child. Then, he denied Christ two more times.

Shortly thereafter, Jesus was crucified and dead.

So now Peter couldn't even make things right. You ever been there? You ever wanted to tell someone something or seek reconciliation, but then it was too late? It's a terrible feeling, and Peter was wallowing in it.

He couldn't fix things. He couldn't apologize for his treachery.

You know, Judas often gets recognized as being the worst disciple. And it's understandable. He sold Jesus out. He betrayed Him.

But let's be real, Judas didn't do anything near as awful

as Peter did. If we were going to rank sins, Peter committed the absolute worst sin a Christ follower can commit. He denied being a disciple. He denied being a friend. He denied even knowing who Jesus was.

It doesn't get any worse than that. That's the low of all lows.

So, Peter is hanging out at rock bottom. And he responded just like a lot of us would; he went fishing. He went back to what he knew best. He tried to escape the pain by doing something that brought him comfort.

He goes back to his old boat and his old net, and he tries to forget.

But just like life, he goes out and fishes all night and doesn't catch a single fish. The professional fisherman doesn't catch a thing.

Talk about being kicked when you're already down.

Then, a man calls out from the shore, "Did you catch anything?"

Thanks random guy. Like Peter didn't already feel bad enough, you have to remind him he's a fishing failure.

Then the man says, "Throw your net on the right side of the boat."

Wow, thanks. Good call. All night they've been trying the left side of the boat when the fish were clearly on the right side. Silly professional fishermen. They didn't know.

I imagine Peter was a little annoyed by what seemed like sarcasm from the man on the shore. But at this point, they didn't have anything to lose, so they dropped their net on the right side of the boat.

And caught an insane number of fish....

Wait, what? Who is this man on the shore?

They realize it's Jesus, and Peter jumps in the water to swim to shore.

When he gets there, one of the most amazing things in all of human history is happening.

Jesus is cooking breakfast.

Just think about that for a moment. Jesus, who by His very nature is God, is making toast. Jesus—the risen from the grave, king of kings, creator of the universe— is on a beach cooking breakfast. He could literally be anywhere in the entire universe, and He's on a beach cooking breakfast.

And to top it off, He's cooking breakfast for a man that just a few days before denied even knowing Him.

Just look at the love of God.

Look at His love, mercy, and forgiveness on display.

And note that Jesus came to Peter.

Peter couldn't restore himself. Peter couldn't fix what he had broken.

All Peter could do is feel sorry for himself and go

fishing.

But Jesus comes, and the first thing he says is, "Children, do you have any fish?"

Did you catch that? He said "children." He's using a family term. He's telling Peter that he may have done wrong, he may have screwed things up, but he is still a son. He is still a part of the family.

Jesus goes to this depressed and broken man, and He cooks him breakfast.

What God is this? I don't know very many people who would even cross the street to do something like this. But yet, Jesus would go to the ends of the earth and beyond just to sit down and cook breakfast.

Then, Jesus restores Peter. He reinstates him.

So, maybe you're at a point in your life where you know you've done some stupid things. Maybe you've made some big mistakes and felt some big consequences. Maybe you've done some things that have made you want to just get away from it all and go fishing.

I get it. I've been there.

Maybe you really want to serve and help others, but there are some things in your past that you think disqualify you. Maybe there are some things you are so ashamed of, and you're having a hard time moving forward.

If that's the case, I want to encourage you to let Jesus

cook for you. He's sitting right there. He's got the toast buttered and everything. And there's a smile on His face as He's saying, "Come, have breakfast."

Let Him restore you.

4

CHANGE A DAY

Therefore do not worry about tomorrow, for tomorrow will worry about itself. Each day has enough trouble of its own.

-Matthew 6:34

When I was living in Los Angeles, there was a moment when my entire perspective on missions changed.

I was working in a homeless shelter, and I had been to Skid Row which is basically the mecca of homelessness in our country. I had met people in heartbreaking situations. I had smelled the rundown hotels and sidewalks where people slept. I had seen folks passed out in the gutter. I had heard story after gut wrenching story of pain and loss and brokenness.

And I've got to be honest, the weight of those burdens was killing me.

A friend took me up to a high hill close to his house, and we looked out over the city.

I could see the Hollywood sign. I could see the ocean and the beaches. I could see the airplanes as they circled the area and came in to land. I could see Santa Monica to Inglewood to Compton to Long Beach to everything in between.

And I thought about how many millions and millions of people were in just the area I could see.

I wondered how many of them were struggling with some terrible situation. I wondered how many of them were hurting. I wondered how many of them were broken. I wondered how many of them were in desperate need of Jesus.

And then I wondered how someone like me could ever hope to make an impact here.

Even if I spent the rest of my life devoted to this city, how many people would I ever be able to talk to?

How many lives could I change compared to how many were in dire need?

I remember feeling very…

very…

small.

But then it happened.

As I looked out over the city of Angels, a quiet voice sounded in the back of my head.

"**Just change a day**," it said. "I'll change lives. You just

KEEP THE FIRE GOING

change someone's day."

My burden was immediately lifted.

It wasn't up to me to change someone's life. That's God's business.

He was calling me to change a person's day. To make them laugh. To encourage them. To inspire them.

And to do everything in my power to help make today better than yesterday.

God would take care of the rest.

And it occurred to me that if enough people changed enough days, some absolutely amazing things would happen.

A while back, I was with a group of high school students in downtown Atlanta. We were making pancakes and inviting all of our residentially challenged friends in to join us for brunch.

A tall, older man named Clark came in, and two of the students found out it was his birthday. So they ran into the kitchen, made a big stack of pancakes, and scrounged around for some birthday candles.

The students lit the candles and brought the pancakes out to Clark. There were about seventy people in the room, and everyone stopped and sang "happy birthday."

Tears streamed down Clark's face.

He blew out the candles and everyone clapped.

A while later, when Clark got up to leave, I stopped him at the door and asked him how old he was that day.

He said 60.

Then I asked, "When's the last time someone sang you happy birthday?"

He thought for a little bit and said, "I think I was 15 the last time someone did that for me."

45 years.

It had been 45 years since someone had said, "Clark, it's your day. And since it's your day, we're gonna light some candles and sing you happy birthday."

45 years.

Did those birthday pancakes change Clark's life? Probably not. Did they change Clark's day?

Absolutely.

And it all started with two high school students seeing an opportunity to love someone.

It's so easy to get wrapped up in the notion of changing lives. And I get it. It sounds good. It feels good. It comes from a good heart and a genuine desire to help people and make the world a better place.

There's nothing wrong with those things.

But the problem is that we often find ourselves only working toward the grand gestures.

We want to donate a million dollars.

We want to drill 100 wells in Africa.

We want to cure cancer.

We want to save the children and feed the hungry and clothe the naked.

And these are amazing and awesome and wonderful things.

But the problem is that **everyone wants to change the world, but no one wants to wash the dishes.**

Changing the world happens one moment at a time. It happens by washing one dish at a time. By saying one kind word at a time. By giving one hug at a time.

It's not about grand gestures and giant unbelievable acts. It's about just trying to change someone's day. And then doing it again the next day and the next day...

Then, before you know it, you look around and crazy unbelievable things have happened. But you get there one day and one moment at a time.

C.S. Lewis once said, "Isn't it funny how day by day nothing changes, but when you look back everything is different."

So, you want to change the world?

Start by helping your mom wash the dishes.

You want to save the children?

Start by getting to know some of the kids in your neighborhood.

You want to feed the hungry?

Start by buying someone lunch.

I think you see what I'm getting at.

I'll leave you with one more story.

A few years ago, I was with some students hanging out with people who live on the street. We were there for a while, sharing a meal, and just talking.

This one student sat and talked to a lady named Susan for about an hour. Susan had been on the streets for years, and the student sat and listened attentively as Susan shared story after story.

Eventually, it was time for us to go, so we started cleaning up and getting ready to leave.

The student thanked Susan for joining us and asked if she could give her a hug.

Susan smiled and held her arms out, and the student closed the gap.

Now, Susan was probably expecting a typical halfway, leave room for Jesus embrace that qualifies more as awkward touching than it does a hug.

26

But this high school girl actually knew how to hug.

She pulled Susan in close and held on tight for at least ten seconds.

When she let go, Susan was crying.

The student panicked a bit and was afraid she had squeezed too tightly.

But then Susan said with a beautiful smile, "No one has hugged me like that in over three years."

Now, it would be naive to think that that hug changed Susan's life, but I guarantee you it changed her day. It might have even changed a few days.

And it's the simplest things that will change the world.

It's hugs and kind words and laughter and washing dishes that will lead to the world becoming a better place.

Grand gestures are awesome. But please remember that they're built by a million little things that don't seem like much.

So, how can you change someone's day today? How can you bring laughter, joy, and encouragement to a person who needs it?

I promise if we set out to change days, God will do some awesome things to change lives.

5

US AND THEM

Love your neighbor as yourself.

-Matthew 22:39

Love your enemies.

-Matthew 5:44

All throughout life, and especially while doing mission work, it's really easy to get into an "us and them" mentality.

There's "us" with our matching t-shirts with the name of our church across the front and "them" wearing whatever they could find in the donation bin at the shelter.

There's "us" who are ready to serve and "them" who we think are in desperate need of us serving them.

There's "us" who have made "right" decisions and "them" who have made "wrong" decisions.

There's "us" who have and "them" who have-not.

Us and them. Us and them. Us and them.

But what's interesting about Jesus is that He only broke people down into two categories. Our neighbors. And our enemies.

And both of which, He told us to love.

The truth of the matter is that there is no "them."

According to Jesus, there are no "others." There are no "those people." It's all people, and they either fit into the neighbors group or the enemies group, and either way, you treat them the same. Love.

If there's anything I've found to be true, it's that people are people. No matter where you go or what you're doing, people are still people.

It doesn't matter if you're under a bridge in Atlanta or in the Ritz Carlton in Chicago or in a refugee camp in Africa or in a mosque in India or in a rice field in Asia.

We all want someone to care. We all want someone to talk to. We all desire community. We all have hopes and dreams and passions and abilities and desires. And most importantly, we all want someone to love us.

Please keep that in the forefront of your mind when you serve, or better yet, keep it on your mind during life in general.

That person at your school no one likes. Just a person.

That lady digging in a dumpster for food. Just a

person.

That stockbroker with not enough time to say excuse me. Just a person.

That little, old lady who cuts you off on the interstate. Just a person.

That smelly guy in the cubicle across from you. Just a person.

That person in the mirror. Just a person.

People are people. Now, let's go love them.

6

A THOUSAND WORDS

Do nothing from rivalry or conceit, but in humility count others more significant than yourselves. Let each of you look not only to his own interests, but also to the interests of others.

-Philippians 2:3-4

A few years ago, I was with a group of students in downtown Atlanta. We were going to different overpasses where many of the city's homeless live, and we were passing out food, prayer, and conversation. We were also working with a local ministry that specializes in getting people into rehab and stable housing.

Two mission teams were there that day. My group and a team led by a pastor I had never met before. There were probably thirty of us in total, so we broke up into three groups to be a little less intimidating.

A couple hours later, we all met back up and headed back to the church where we were staying. As we rode in the church van, the students were telling each other about the people they met and the conversations they had. A couple people had decided to come off of the streets, so they were definitely excited about that.

But then someone said, "Can you believe how that guy was taking pictures?"

I turned around. "Who was taking pictures?" I asked. The students knew how I felt about pictures. I had made it quite clear that this isn't poverty tourism. We were neither at the zoo nor on safari. And if you were gonna take a picture of a man experiencing homelessness, you better be in the picture and you better know the person's name and part of his story, and you better be dang sure that he's alright with it.

"It was the pastor from the other group," a girl said. "He was all up in people's faces with this giant camera."

"Did anybody say anything to him?" I asked.

A young man said, "I asked him if he had permission from the people to take their picture, and he said, 'Permission? These people should just be happy I'm here.'"

I'm gonna chalk it up to the grace of God that I was not in the group with that pastor. I don't think it would have gone well. I'm not saying I would have tossed him into oncoming traffic or anything, but he and I would have had a long conversation, and there's a chance he would've needed to buy a new camera.

He was the great, white hope there to save the day. And he had to make sure to document every second of saving the poor, pitiful homeless men. He had to make sure his congregation knew how spiritual he was as I'm sure those pictures wound up in a slideshow set to sappy music that played during that next Sunday morning's service.

But whose good was that pastor really seeking?

Was he really there to serve others, or was it about serving his own ego?

It's so easy to make things about ourselves. Humans are naturally talented at being self-serving and self-centered. And we can easily fall into the same egotistical trap that pastor did if we're not careful.

The old cliché is that a picture is worth a thousand words, but when serving others we need to guard against the urge to capture every moment on our phones. It needs to be more about the thousand words than the pictures. We need to talk to people and build relationships.

And we need to do this at the detriment of our social media accounts. Serving others should be about transforming more than just our profile pictures.

We have to seek the good of others, and that means not exploiting their poverty or situation with photo ops.

What if I walked in your house one afternoon and started taking pictures? What if I made sure to take pictures of your dirty underwear and dirty dishes?

What if I picked up members of your family and posed while my friends took my picture? What if I was there for ten minutes and left without so much as asking you your name?

That would be super weird and offensive, right?

Yet, that's pretty much what people constantly do while serving.

Please, leave the phone in your pocket. Leave the camera at home.

Let go of the photos, and start pursuing the thousand words.

7

KEEP KNOCKING

So we must not get tired of doing good, for we will reap at the proper time if we don't give up.

-Galatians 6:9

We've established that it's God's business to change lives and that we just need to focus on changing people's days.

But what about when changing someone's day is hard?

Really hard.

Like, want to slam your head in a car door hard.

I mean, let's just be honest, sometimes people need a high five.

In the face.

With a chair.

But what do we do in those moments when we really

just want to give up?

How do we handle things when people test our patience, break our trust, and deserve to be given up on?

We keep knocking.

Yeah, I know, it's easy for me to say. I don't know your friend. I don't know your family member. I don't know the person you've been trying to help for years that just consistently screws things up.

And you're right. I don't know the people in your life.

But I do know a guy named John.

John was one of those people that you can set your watch by. He did the same exact things everyday at the exact same times.

He was homeless, but he knew where to find food and where to find a place to sleep.

He also knew where to find a liquor store.

John hadn't always been like this. He had had a wife. He had had a family.

But some really tough circumstances had left John homeless, and after a while he got tired of trying, and he basically just gave up.

He started using alcohol to numb the pain and help him forget about the situation he found himself in.

And John slowly spiraled down until he landed in a

tragic cycle that kept him trapped in a tragic routine.

Everyday was the same.

He would wake up at the homeless shelter. Eat breakfast. And leave.

Then, he would sit outside for a while.

And sit.

And sit.

At noon, he would walk over to the soup kitchen and eat lunch.

Then, he would sit outside for a while.

Except this time he sat on a street corner holding a sign and asking people for money.

Some days people gave. Some days they didn't.

Some days John got drunk. Some days he didn't.

Then, he would make his way back to the homeless shelter. Check in. Eat dinner. And go to sleep.

The next morning, he would do it all over again.

It was clockwork. It was robotic. It was John's entire existence.

But there was one other thing that was the exact same everyday: the people who worked at the shelter.

The shelter had a rehab program and a job program. It

had classes to help people get back on their feet and reconnect with their families. It had a way for people to find a better life.

And everyday, someone from the shelter would invite John into the program. Someone would love on him. Someone would give him a hug. Someone would offer an encouraging word.

Every.

Single.

Day.

Over and over again.

And everyday, John would smile and thank them for the offer, and then he would decline and go back to his routine.

Every.

Single.

Day.

Over and over again.

Then, one day, the director of the shelter walked into the large dining hall where hundreds of homeless men were eating, and he scanned the room.

But today, he noticed something strange. John was sitting at a table reserved for men in the rehab program. The director was puzzled, so he walked over to the table.

"John," he said jokingly, "did you finally decide to get in the program?"

"I did," John said.

The director was stunned. He couldn't believe it. He grabbed John's shoulders and looked him right in the eyes. "Why?" he asked. "What makes today any different?"

"Today is the hundredth day," John said casually.

"What do you mean?" Now the director was really confused.

John continued, "Today is the hundredth day in a row that I came in here and someone invited me into this program." He wiped his mouth. "And after a hundred days, I figured you guys really did want me here."

The director smiled. "You couldn't have believed us after thirty days?"

"Nope, had to be a hundred," John said. "And let's just be honest, there were a lot of days when I didn't deserve to be invited in. A lot of days I showed up drunk and belligerent. A lot of days I said things I shouldn't have and didn't treat people very well. But still, every single day, someone made it a point to talk to me and show me kindness."

Here's the thing about helping people: **We never know what day we're on.**

We never know if it's day one, and kindness is just starting to make an impact.

We never know if it's day forty-seven, and compassion is just keeping someone going.

And we never know if it's day one hundred, and one more act of love is just what someone needs to show them that there's hope.

That's why it's so important to keep knocking.

Day after day.

Over and over again.

Paul tells us to not get tired of doing good. He says that if we just keep knocking, eventually amazing things will happen.

He tells us to not give up.

Even when it's hard.

Even when it makes more sense.

Even when it seems like the smart thing to do.

We must not give up.

We have to keep knocking.

And we have to believe that God will move in mighty ways to open the doors we're knocking on.

Now, let me make it abundantly clear that I'm not talking about people that abuse you. I am not encouraging you to stay in a harmful relationship or with toxic people. That is a totally different situation.

And I think you know the difference.

This is about the people God has placed in your life that need someone to love them. The people that need an advocate. The people that need someone to fight for them.

The people that need someone to just keep knocking on their door.

And I'm willing to bet that **you're where you are because someone kept knocking on your door.**

I know that's the case with me.

Lord knows, there have been times in my life when people should have given up on me.

But they didn't.

No matter how bad things got. No matter how much I screwed things up. Someone kept knocking.

Someone kept loving me.

Someone kept encouraging me.

Someone kept fighting for me.

A lot of people walked away. A lot of people threw in the towel. A lot of people decided it wasn't worth it.

But I am where I am because of the few who kept knocking even when everyone else walked away.

And it's probably the same for you.

And we can all agree that Jesus keeps knocking no matter what.

So, who's door can you knock on today?

What friend or family member just needs someone to love on them right now?

What person in your life just needs someone to fight for them and show them some compassion and kindness?

8

POWER OF PRAYER

The prayer of a righteous person is powerful and effective.

-James 5:16

I met a man named Gary a while back. He was living in a shelter and going through a program to help him get back on his feet. He's a very joyful guy with a great laugh, and one day he told me how he ended up there.

Gary had struggled with smoking crack for years. He would do it for a while and then quit for a while.

He tried to break the habit time and time again, but he always found himself lighting up again.

One day, during a period of sobriety, he cried out to God to take the taste out of his mouth for drugs. He really wanted to get his life back together, and he knew that was his biggest obstacle.

After praying that prayer, things went well for a while.

But then the urge to smoke overtook him again, and he wound up at the same street corner he always bought from. After buying the drugs, he made his way over to his favorite spot to get high, and smoked it all up.

Then, he waited...and waited...and waited.

But nothing happened. He didn't get high.

Well, this made Gary upset. He assumed the dealer had sold him bad stuff, so he went to the dealer and cussed him out.

Then, he called up another dealer, and bought more crack.

He went back to his spot and smoked all of it. But again, nothing happened.

So now he's really upset. He goes back to that dealer and cusses him out.

Then, he calls a third dealer and goes through the exact same process and has the exact same result.

Gary ends up sitting on a curb on the side of the road. He's sober. He's frustrated. He's annoyed. He can't figure out what's going on. And he's out of money.

And in that moment, a voice whispers in the back of his head, "Remember what you prayed? I took the taste out of your mouth."

Then, it hits Gary what he had cried out to God about months earlier.

His prayer had been answered. The next day, he checked himself into a treatment program to start getting his life back together.

In scripture, James tells us the prayer of a righteous person is powerful and effective.

And Gary will definitely tell you that's the truth. He experienced it firsthand.

9

LEARN THE LANGUAGE

Now there were staying in Jerusalem God-fearing Jews from every nation under heaven. When they heard this sound, a crowd came together in bewilderment, because each one heard their own language being spoken. Utterly amazed, they asked: "Aren't all these who are speaking Galileans? Then how is it that each of us hears them in our native language? Parthians, Medes and Elamites; residents of Mesopotamia, Judea and Cappadocia, Pontus and Asia, Phrygia and Pamphylia, Egypt and the parts of Libya near Cyrene; visitors from Rome (both Jews and converts to Judaism); Cretans and Arabs—we hear them declaring the wonders of God in our own tongues!" Amazed and perplexed, they asked one another, "What does this mean?"

-Acts 2:5-12

My wife and I spend the majority of the year in Honduras. We are currently foster parents for two beautiful little girls that we are also in the process of adopting.

When our oldest daughter came to live with us, she was five years old and didn't know a word of English.

This wasn't a big deal for my wife because she's fluent in Spanish. She's so good that there are times when the Hondurans can't tell she's an American.

At the time, however, I did not fit into that category. I only had a basic understanding of the language meaning that I could greet someone, say thank you, and ask where the bathroom was, but that was about it.

One night, my wife was busy cooking dinner, so she asked me to brush our daughters' hair when they got done bathing. Our oldest finished first, so in what I thought was pretty good Spanish for a guy from Alabama, I told her to go to her room and bring me her comb.

My wife burst out laughing.

Fall down, roll around, and tear up kind of laughing.

I was confused.

My daughter stared at me. She was more perplexed than I was.

I asked my wife what happened.

Through her laughter, she told me that my Spanish had been good except for one word. She informed me that my pronunciation of the word for comb was wrong.

I was a little frustrated. Why was that so funny?

She wiped tears from her eyes and told me that I had just told our daughter to go to her room and bring me her penis.

That's right.

I had just said the Spanish word for penis to my five-year-old daughter.

Apparently, it's only one letter different than the word for comb. And that's just bad language development, if you ask me.

After that extremely embarrassing moment, I decided to make learning Spanish a much higher priority. I'm still nowhere near fluent, but I can communicate effectively, and I've never screwed up the word for comb again.

It's so important to speak the language of the people we're serving.

But please understand, **I'm talking about something much bigger than words.**

This is about culture, taboos, history, expectations, past experiences, and a host of other things.

I grew up in a small town full of blue-collar people. They spoke a certain language.

I played football in high school and college. My

coaches and teammates spoke a certain language.

I worked for a big church in a wealthy community. Those people spoke a certain language.

I served at an orphanage in Honduras. The staff spoke a certain language. The children spoke a certain language.

In every situation, the people and culture you're around are going to say and do specific things based on countless different reasons.

And too often, we go into situations without understanding the language of the people we're serving, and we end up doing more harm than good.

A lot of times we believe the way we do things is best, so everyone else should do things the way we do them.

We would probably never say that, of course. But our actions prove it.

I've talked with leaders from other countries, and many of them have said the same thing. The Americans always think they know better. They talk the loudest and usually have the last word.

For a lot of years, mission trips were basically a form of colonialism. We claimed to have other people's best interests in mind, but we were really just trying to make them more like us.

And the same thing is true for many neighborhoods and communities in the United States. A group of people came in to "help," but they had certain expectations of how the people being served should behave and respond.

I think people have meant well—they've truly wanted to help and love others—but they made no effort to understand the culture, history, and day-to-day struggles of the people they were trying to help.

And in doing so, many people have been hurt, offended, and disrespected as they were told that they spoke the wrong language. As they were told their culture was inferior. As they were told the way they do things was less than.

If we really want to help people, we have to have at least a basic understanding of where they're coming from.

And we have to stop assuming our way is best.

When it comes to culture, often times, there is no best way.

Certain things in certain communities work better than others, sure, but it's all so wrapped up in history, past experiences, and a million other things, it's impossible to determine a "best" way.

I have a friend that's spent a great deal of time in Kenya. For years, he's worked with different villages to do everything from drill wells and build schools to train leaders and build churches.

But a while back, he and I were talking about all the effort so many mission teams and organizations had put into the area. He was telling me about all the changes he had seen happen over a ten-year span. He had seen some truly amazing things take place in those villages.

But he had also seen some not so great things, and he made a truly sobering statement:

"Sometimes, I'm afraid that instead of helping them to be more like Jesus, we've really just helped them to be more like us."

The people's lives had definitely improved, but they had also become more materialistic. They had better access to healthcare and clean water, but they also complained more and acted more selfishly.

They had been modernized but also Americanized.

That's why it's so important to learn the language of the people we're serving. But it's got to be more than learning what they say and do. We have to learn why they say and do it.

We have to see things from their perspective.

As Jesus followers, it's not up to us to "fix" people's culture. It's up to us to love people like Jesus.

Trying to "fix" only creates discord, resentment, and indignation. No one likes to be treated like a project. And no one wants to be told his culture is "bad" or "wrong."

Relationships aren't built this way.

So, if you really want to help people, learn their language. But learn **why** they say and do things.

And the best way to do that is to sit and listen.

Don't tell people what they need. Let them tell you.

And make sure to learn how to pronounce words that sound similar to body parts

The Monkey and the Fish

A storm had temporarily stranded a monkey on an island.

In a secure, protected place on the shore, while waiting for the raging waters to recede, he noticed a fish swimming against the current. It seemed obvious to the monkey that the fish was struggling and needed help. Being of kind heart, the monkey resolved to help the fish.

A tree precariously dangled over the very spot where the fish seemed to be struggling.

At a considerable risk to himself, the monkey moved far out on a limb, reached down and snatched the fish from the threatening waters. Immediately scurrying back to the safety of his shelter, he carefully laid the fish on dry ground.

For a few moments, the fish showed excitement, but soon settled into a peaceful rest. Joy and satisfaction swelled inside the monkey.

He had successfully helped another creature.

I ran across this story a while back, and I think it paints a perfect picture of what mission work so often looks like.

So often, we go in with the best intentions and end up doing more harm than good.

The desire to serve and help others is wonderful, but we have to make sure we're actually helping and not hurting. We have to make sure we're empowering people and not enabling. We have to make sure we're giving hand ups and not just handouts.

And the only way to accomplish this is to build relationships. It's only through relationships that we can truly find ways to help people. Because it's through relationships that we find out what people really need. And it's through relationships that we set others up for long-term success as opposed to setting ourselves up for short-term feelings of accomplishment.

To do things the right way, the monkey has to jump in the water and swim alongside the fish. He has to see life from under the water. He has to let the fish show him the way.

10

WHAT'S IN A NAME

When Jesus reached the spot, he looked up and said to him, "Zacchaeus, come down immediately. I must stay at your house today." So he came down at once and welcomed him gladly.

All the people saw this and began to mutter, "He has gone to be the guest of a sinner."

But Zacchaeus stood up and said to the Lord, "Look, Lord! Here and now I give half of my possessions to the poor, and if I have cheated anybody out of anything, I will pay back four times the amount."

Jesus said to him, "Today salvation has come to this house, because this man, too, is a son of Abraham. For the Son of Man came to seek and to save the lost."

-Luke 19:5-10

During my first week of college, I met a girl named Anna. She was smart and funny and really pretty. The night I met her, we had an awesome conversation about everything from sports to faith, and we talked for over an hour.

This girl captivated me.

The next day, during lunch, I ran into her in the big dining hall on campus. I said, "Hey, Anna!" with obvious excitement.

And she replied, "Heyyyyy, buddy…"

She had forgotten my name.

I was crushed.

Our names are such interesting things. We don't think about it often, but having people know our names is really important.

A few years ago, some friends and I met a man on the street named James. He was a really cool guy going through a rehab program at a shelter, and every time we went downtown to serve, we would see James and hang out with him.

One time, we found out that James' birthday was the next day, so we went home that night and made him a big batch of cookies.

We put the cookies in a Styrofoam take-out box and wrote "JAMES" on the lid.

The next day, we traveled downtown to find James. When we saw him, we sang happy birthday and I handed him the box of cookies.

He stared at the box.

He looked at us and smiled.

Then, he stared at the box again.

"That's my name," he said pointing to the lid.

I said, "There's some really good cookies in there..."

"Yeah, but that's my name," he replied. "This belongs to me."

James was more excited to have his name on the box than he was to have the cookies.

There's just something special about people knowing your name. This is especially true for people in tough situations.

A homeless man doesn't hear his name often. In the shelter system, he's a bed number. On the street, people treat him like he's invisible. The few people who actually know him probably don't know his real name.

An orphan gets lost in the sea of other children. She has a name on a file, but she's just one of many. She's a case number.

A prisoner is a number on his jumpsuit. He's remembered more for what he did than for who he is.

A widow's name is slowly forgotten as more and more people who know her pass away.

We have to learn people's names. We have to get to

know them and build relationships.

People need a lot more than our used clothes; they need our presence. They need us to be part of their lives.

The first thing Jesus says to Zacchaeus is his name. Jesus stops, looks up in a tree, and says "Zacchaeus."

Can you imagine what that must have been like for the tax collector?

Tax collectors were at the bottom of Jewish society. They had a lot of money, but they got it all by cheating their fellow Jews and collecting taxes for the Roman Empire.

They were outcasts. The only time people used their names was to criticize them.

But then Jesus, a rabbi and man of God, knows exactly who Zacchaeus is, calls him by name, and wants to come over for dinner.

What? That's crazy.

Then, Zacchaeus ends up having one of the most remarkable conversions of anyone in all of scripture. After receiving salvation, he gives away half of his possessions to the poor and pays back everyone he ever cheated with interest.

And how did Jesus start this process?

By saying the man's name.

As people, we all have the innate desire to be known. We want others to know who we are and to know our names.

So, if we really want to help people, we have to get to know them.

Passing out sandwiches and saying "God bless" isn't enough.

We have to be present in people's lives. We have to know their names and their stories, and they have to know ours.

It's through relationship that lives are changed.

11

GET ON HER LEVEL

Truly I tell you, anyone who will not receive the kingdom of God like a little child will never enter it.

-Mark 10:15

When it gets really cold, my church opens its gym up for the homeless to come in and have a warm place to sleep.

We always have tons of volunteers there helping with everything from serving food to setting up air mattresses to just sitting down and talking with folks.

It's truly one of my favorite things the church does because it brings so many people together, and it's a great moment for the church and its entire congregation to live out Matthew 25:40.

On those nights, we always get flooded with lots of donations, so we put giant, yellow barrels out in front of the gym for people to drop off blankets, sheets, pillows, and etc.

One night, I was emptying one of the barrels when a minivan pulled up.

The middle door slid open and a little girl jumped out with her arms full of blankets.

She gleefully ran over to where I was standing and stopped. She looked at me. She looked at the barrel. She looked at me. And then she tossed the blankets in the barrel and ran back to the van.

At this point, I wasn't entirely sure what had just happened. I felt like I had been part of the cutest drive-by to ever occur in Atlanta.

About that time, the girl's mother got out of the car, and her arms were full of even more blankets.

She walked over, dropped them in the barrel, and said, "It's Elizabeth's birthday today, but instead of asking her friends for presents, she asked them to give blankets to the homeless."

As the minivan drove away, I heard a voice whisper in the back of my head, "Get on her level."

It's always fun when an eight year old makes you feel convicted.

I had to check my heart. Was I willing to be as selfless as she had been? Would I give up the day that's supposed to be about me and instead make it about loving and helping someone else? Was I seeing people the way that God saw them?

These are questions we all need to ask ourselves. And I want to tell you the same thing God told me. **Get on her level**.

12

BE INTERRUPTIBLE

They forced a man coming in from the country, who was passing by, to carry Jesus' cross. He was Simon, a Cyrenian, the father of Alexander and Rufus. And they brought Jesus to the place called Golgotha (which means Skull Place).

-Mark 15:21-22

So, imagine you're on your way into the city. You're running a little late. You've got a lot on your mind. You've got important business to take care of. And to top it off, you've got your two kids to keep track of.

Then, out of nowhere, a giant crowd of people shows up and blocks your path. Jews and Roman soldiers are yelling and spitting. They're saying things you wish your kids weren't hearing.

And in the midst of the crowd is a man.

A bloody, broken, disfigured, torn apart man.

And he's obviously the focus of the crowd's attention.

You watch as the man does his best to carry a large wooden support beam. You realize it's for a Roman cross. This man is on his way to be crucified.

Maybe you wonder what he did to deserve to die. Maybe you don't. Your mind is really on what you came to the city to do. You don't get many opportunities to come to the city, and you have to get back home before nightfall. It's imperative that you not lose any more time.

You see the man collapse under the beam. He's exhausted. You can't believe he made it this far.

The people start yelling even more. A soldier kicks him and screams for him to get up.

It bothers you a little bit how they're treating this man. But, at the same time, he's a criminal. He deserves to be treated this way. He should have thought twice before doing whatever he did.

You sigh impatiently. You really need to get by. You don't have time for this.

But then a soldier turns and looks at the crowd. He's looking for someone. His eyes meet yours.

"You!" he yells. "Come here!"

You take a step back. Surely, he's not talking to you. You hold your hands out to the side and guide your kids behind you.

The soldier walks over to you and grabs your shirt. "Carry the cross," he says gruffly.

KEEP THE FIRE GOING

You want to say no, but you know you can't. This is a Roman soldier. He can make you do anything he wants.

You nod your head and look down at your children. You tell them to stay close as you walk over to the man and crossbeam.

As you take hold of the beam, the man looks up at you. He's covered in dust and blood. His eyes are almost swollen shut. But as you make eye contact, something happens.

The hair stands up on the back of your neck, and a wave of peace washes over you.

Who is this man?

A soldier pushes you. He's got his own appointments to keep.

You pick up the crossbeam, and the man rises to his feet. He grabs your arm to keep his balance, and you feel something pulse through your body. This is no ordinary criminal. He's something different.

The two of you slowly walk to the outskirts of the city. You know where you're going.

Golgotha.

The skull place.

The place where thieves, murderers, and rebels go to die.

As you arrive, you see two other men already there being crucified. Soldiers come and take the crossbeam from you. They grab the man and throw him to the ground.

With hammer and nails, they put him on the cross.

Your children walk up and grab your hands. The three of you watch as the man is crucified.

A few days later, word gets to you that a man has risen from the dead. A friend from the city tells you all about a man named Jesus and how he was crucified, dead, and buried. And about how he had come back from the grave.

You can't explain it, but you know it's the same man that walked beside you.

Your friend asks if you knew of Jesus.

You smile and say, "I carried His cross."

Simon the Cyrenian was just a regular guy that had come to the city to get something done. He probably just wanted to finish his to-do list, grab some lunch, and head back home.

But he was interrupted.

Jesus crossed his path and changed his plans.

We often talk about carrying metaphorical crosses. Simon carried it for real.

What an incredible honor that was. And at the time,

Simon had no idea how big a deal it actually was.

And that's usually how it works.

We'll be on our way to do something when an opportunity to help someone will pop up. We'll be on our way to work or trying to study for a test or running late for an appointment when, out of the blue, Jesus will cross our paths.

And it's in those moments that we have an opportunity to choose between our schedules and carrying the cross.

I want to encourage you to be interruptible. Be okay when things pop up and schedules change. You might be in the midst of something special without realizing it.

In Romans 16, Paul sends a special greeting to a man named Rufus. Many Bible scholars believe it to be the same Rufus that is mentioned as being the son of Simon who carried Jesus' cross.

Most of the disciples weren't there for the crucifixion. But Rufus was. He walked next to Jesus as he went to his death. He watched his father carry Jesus' cross. And he stood next to his family as Jesus was nailed into place.

And it seemed to have a pretty big impact on his life as he went on to become an influential part of the early church.

So, whenever Jesus crosses your path, I hope you'll

stop to spend time with Him. Whenever inconvenient and bothersome things arise in your life, I hope you'll realize that there might be something bigger going on.

Whenever you're interrupted, I hope you'll see it as potentially being a grand honor in disguise.

13

WHEN GIANTS COME ALONG

Now Jesse said to his son David, "Take this ephah of roasted grain and these ten loaves of bread for your brothers and hurry to their camp. Take along these ten cheeses to the commander of their unit. See how your brothers are and bring back some assurance from them. They are with Saul and all the men of Israel in the Valley of Elah, fighting against the Philistines."

-1st Samuel 17:17-19

The church I work for sends a mission team to Honduras every year to serve at an orphanage. A few years back, the team was getting ready to go and the church's missions pastor, my boss, was going to lead them.

However, three days before the team left, the missions pastor had to back out.

I remember the day well because it's the same day I was told to clear my schedule and pack a bag because I was going to take his place. I also needed to prepare a sermon because I was going to be preaching.

I didn't know anything about the trip, and I didn't really know any of the people who were going. All I was told was that I was headed to an orphanage in a third world country.

To be completely honest, I didn't particularly want to go. I was focused on domestic missions at the time and felt zero desire to travel overseas. I was busy and not very excited to spend a week in another country.

But there I was on the church bus headed to the airport at 5AM. I had barely slept. I was hungry and grumpy. And I remember leaning my head up against the bus's cold window and thinking, "God, I don't know what you're doing, but I don't want to be here, so this trip better be cool."

Just for the record, God knows our thoughts, and He has an interesting sense of humor.

On that trip, I met the woman that I eventually married. She was a missionary serving at the orphanage.

She was in the process of adopting one of the children from the orphanage, so on that trip, I met the little girl who is now my daughter.

Come to find out, that little girl has a sister who also lived at the orphanage, so on that trip, I also met the other little girl who is now my daughter.

And as I write this, I'm currently living and serving in

Honduras.

Ha ha, ha ha says the Lord.

I didn't set out to do anything but fill in on a mission trip that my boss had to back out of. And to be fair, I didn't even want to do that.

But there are times when Goliath walks in front of you and changes everything.

David was just a young man watching his father's sheep while his brothers went off to war. His father packed up some food and told him to take it to his brothers.

So he set off to do a very simple task. His whole mission was to deliver bread and cheese.

But when David arrived to the camp, there was a giant named Goliath there yelling obscenities.

David hadn't left home that day thinking he'd go to war. He carried bread, not a sword. He hadn't set off thinking his entire life was going to change by that afternoon.

But a giant stood before him, and David felt compelled by God to do something about him. And one well-placed rock later everything was different.

And that's so often how life goes.

As you get into serving the people of your community, you're going to run into problems and needs that you didn't see coming.

And some of those problems are going to be giant.

But it's those unexpected giants that come along and change everything.

14

GOOD NEWS

And there were shepherds living out in the fields nearby, keeping watch over their flocks at night. An angel of the Lord appeared to them, and the glory of the Lord shone around them, and they were terrified. But the angel said to them, "Do not be afraid. I bring you good news that will cause great joy for all the people. Today in the town of David a Savior has been born to you; he is the Messiah, the Lord.

-Luke 2:8-11

My mother isn't supposed to be able to have children. It was just a fact of life.

She had been pregnant once, but due to tragic complications, the baby died during delivery. After that, my mother's doctor said she would never be able to get pregnant again.

Seven years later, my mother got very sick. She was having lots of stomach problems and pain in her abdomen.

Finally, it got to be too much, so she went to the doctor. After running some tests, her doctor informed her of some very bad news. He believed the pain and sickness were being caused by a tumor and that it might be cancerous.

Her doctor said he was going to send her to a specialist for more testing and to pack some extra clothes because there was a good chance she was going to need surgery immediately.

My mother was shocked. A few days before, life was normal and everything was fine. And now, all of a sudden, she might have a large, cancerous tumor that requires life-threatening surgery.

The next day, she went to the specialist to have more tests done. She gripped her bag of extra clothes tightly as she sat in the waiting room. Was it cancer? Does it require surgery? Today? Is this how it all ends?

The doctor finally walked out. He had a stern look on his face as he stared at a paper with the test results.

He said, "It's not cancer."

My mother sighed with huge relief.

"It's not even a tumor," he continued.

Now my mother was confused and scared again.

"You're pregnant," he said.

My mother laughed. "That's impossible," she said.

The doctor handed her the test results. "Then this is impossibly good news."

Later that year, my mother gave birth to me.

What they thought was a cancerous tumor turned out to be good news that brought great joy.

Do you ever wonder why the angel appeared to a bunch of random shepherds to tell them about Jesus?

For a long time, I just figured God was drawing some parallels. They're shepherds. Jesus is going to shepherd His people. He's the sacrificial lamb. You know, all those biblical metaphors.

And while I still think that's part of what God was doing, I've also come to realize there was something much bigger happening here.

And there was an incredible message God was sending to the world as His angels appeared to those shepherds.

Let's just think about the overall profession of being a shepherd.

It was a dirty job. You had to live outside. You had to use the bathroom behind bushes. You had to deliver lambs. You had to walk around in the hot sun all day. You had to fight off wild animals. You had to touch sick animals. You had to touch dead animals. You had to do a lot of things that weren't particularly clean.

And this was a problem for Jewish shepherds because the Law is pretty clear about cleanliness. It goes into great detail about touching animals, blood, sickness, bodily waste, dead things, and lots more.

To follow the Law as a shepherd required a constant effort to make sacrifices and make amends for the laws you were breaking.

The normal duties of your profession basically required breaking the law on a daily basis.

And because of this, Jewish shepherds were outsiders in their society. They were looked down upon by the spiritual elites.

But yet, who do the angels appear to? Who do the angels announce the arrival of Jesus to? Who does God want to make sure is aware of world changing events?

Not the religious elite. Not the people who society says are worthy.

Shepherds.

Unclean.

Law-breaking.

Shepherds.

And the angel says don't be afraid, I have **good news** that will cause great joy.

You're dang right it's good news! It's news that people who cannot possibly follow the law—people who cannot stop being unclean—can be redeemed and made pure by something much bigger than their infinitely failing personal efforts.

It's news that God has sent reconciliation in the form of His son.

It's news that all people will have access to God.

It's news that everyone who has fallen short (which is everyone) will have an opportunity at redemption.

Do you think the shepherds felt great joy over these things?

I bet they were ecstatic.

Later on, in Matthew 5-7, Jesus gives the famous Sermon on the Mount. It's some of the most incredible language as Jesus reveals the true nature of sin, God's people, Himself, and the kingdom of heaven.

Over and over again, Jesus turns commonly held thoughts and beliefs on their heads and explains how things should really be.

And in Matthew 8, something amazing happens.

When Jesus came down from the mountainside, large crowds followed him. A man with leprosy came and knelt before him and said, "Lord, if you are willing, you can make me clean."

Jesus reached out his hand and touched the man. "I am willing," he said. "Be clean!" Immediately he was cleansed of his leprosy.

-Matthew 8:1-3

What I love about Jesus is that He didn't just talk about the kingdom of heaven; he also showed them what it was like. He showed them that things had changed.

According to the law, you can't touch a sick person without being made unclean. You especially can't touch someone with leprosy! This is Jewish law 101. Everyone knows that.

But Jesus reaches out His hand and touches the man.

A man of God touches a leper.

This is insane.

This goes against everything the priests have taught.

When something clean touches something unclean, it becomes unclean. That's just the way it is. You can't transfer cleanliness.

When my children come into my freshly cleaned house, it immediately becomes unclean.

If a doctor scrubs in for surgery and then shakes someone's hand, the doctor's hand becomes compromised. The other person doesn't become clean.

So what Jesus is doing here appears to be law-breaking at its finest.

He's touching a man whose very existence is unclean.

But then the man is healed!

In other words, Jesus does what nothing and no one else can: transfer cleanliness.

And this is good news that causes great joy.

All the dirty and unclean things of this world can be made clean through Jesus. Or put more clearly, because of Jesus, you and I can be reconciled back to God.

And ultimately, that's the main point of missions—to go out and spread the good news that causes great joy and to make sure people are aware of what Jesus has done for them.

That's why it's so important for us to go out and build relationships with people in our communities, neighborhoods, jobs, schools, and families.

We have good news about the love of God. It has brought us great joy.

Now, let's go make more people aware of it.

15

SMELLY HUG

The King will reply, "Truly I tell you, whatever you did for one of the least of these brothers and sisters of mine, you did for me."

-Matthew 25:40

A while back, I was with some students passing out lunches and praying with people in one of the tough neighborhoods near the Georgia Dome in Atlanta.

Things were going well as people were being fed in their stomachs and their souls.

There was an older man there and after handing him a lunch and praying with him, I reached out to give him a hug.

He pulled me in close and squeezed me pretty tight.

And it was at this point that I realized he was probably

the worst smelling human being I had ever come into contact with.

I didn't want to do or say anything to hurt his feelings, so I held my breath and toughed out the 10 second embrace.

As he walked away, I remember thinking, "Lord, please don't ever let me hug someone who smells that bad again."

I'm not proud of thinking that, but it is what it is.

But then the quiet voice of Jesus sounded in the back of my head, "But that's what I smell like."

My heart immediately felt a great deal of conviction. That wasn't some smelly, toothless, drug addict I had been hugging.

That was Jesus.

Matthew 25:40 doesn't say whenever we do something for someone else, *it's like* we're doing it for Jesus.

It doesn't say it's *as if* we're doing it for Jesus.

No, it specifically states that doing something for someone else is doing it for Jesus Himself.

And it's a privilege to serve and hug Jesus no matter what He smells like.

Just think how the world would change if we treated everyone we met like it was Jesus.

16

WITNESS

For we did not follow cleverly devised stories when we told you about the coming of our Lord Jesus Christ in power, but we were eyewitnesses of his majesty.

-2ⁿᵈ Peter 1:16

I have a friend named Grant. He's a good guy. He grew up in a Christian home. He went to church every chance he could. He went on mission trips. By all accounts, Grant loved Jesus.

But one evening, when Grant was in college, he had his life turned upside down.

He was with his church at a soup kitchen serving dinner. Things were going well. Lots of people were coming in to be fed, and Grant and his church friends were having a good time hanging out in the kitchen.

But something started to bother Grant. There was an obvious divide between the homeless people that were eating and the church people that were serving.

The kitchen was full of laughter while the dining room was somber and quiet.

Grant took his hairnet off and left the kitchen. He got in line and got a plate of food.

When his pastor saw him, he reprimanded Grant. He said Grant was taking food away from someone else.

Grant responded, "I think it might be about more than just the food."

He looked around and found a seat next to a man in a big, orange jacket. The weather was freezing outside.

Grant made small talk with the man as they both chowed down on spaghetti.

The man told Grant about a good thing that had happened to him that day, and Grant responded with, "Man, God is so good."

The man smiled and stared at Grant.

"It's interesting that you say that," the man said. "I say that too."

"Right on," Grant said cheerfully.

The man continued, "But here's the thing. In just a little bit, you're gonna go and get in your car and drive home. You'll take a hot shower, watch some TV, and then crawl into your big, warm, comfortable bed. And you'll say God is good."

Grant started to feel uncomfortable.

The man kept going, "But I'll leave from here and walk two miles in the snow to get to the bridge where I'll be staying for the night. No shower. No TV. No warm bed. And I'll also say God is good."

The man put his hand on Grant's shoulder and said, "I have to wonder. Do you really think God is good, or is He only good based on your circumstances?"

The man got up from the table and left Grant sitting there stunned.

He didn't know. He had grown up reading his Bible and attending worship services. He had put in countless hours serving others. He knew every parable Jesus ever told.

But now, sitting at a table by himself at a soup kitchen, he couldn't answer the question.

Did he really and truly believe in God's goodness or was it really just his circumstances that made him think so.

For the next few months, he couldn't get it out of his head. Was God good?

He had to find out.

He started getting rid of stuff. He sold his Xbox. He gave away his clothes. He sold his car and his furniture.

But it still wasn't enough.

He had to find the answer.

Grant decided that the only way to find out was to give up everything.

So he did.

And then he bought a bus ticket to Florida and started living on the street.

I met Grant about six months later after he had made his way up to Atlanta. He told me this story and a bunch of others about the people he had met and the different adventures he'd had.

When he finished, I asked him, "Well, did you figure it out? Is God good?"

He sighed and smiled. "He's so good," he said.

Grant had become an eyewitness.

He no longer believed in God's goodness based on his circumstances. He no longer believed in Jesus just because he was supposed to. It was no longer about what his parents believed or what he had been told since he was a child.

Now, it was about what he had experienced. Now, he actually owned his faith.

Peter tells us that this whole Jesus thing isn't just a bunch of clever stories put together by men.

He says that he and the other disciples were eyewitnesses to all the things Jesus said and did. He wasn't just spreading metaphors full of fluffy language.

They had literally seen Jesus heal the sick and the blind. They had seen him feed thousands of people with a basket of food. They had seen him raised from the dead.

They were witnesses.

So often, we read about the lives of the disciples, and we talk about how radical their lives were. We think the ways they lived and the ways they died were crazy.

But let's be honest, if we really think about it, their lives weren't really radical at all. After experiencing what they did and seeing all they did, it would have been crazy to not live passionately for the Lord. It would have been crazy to not go out and proclaim the gospel no matter what the consequences would be.

What would have been absolutely crazy is if they had seen Jesus do all those things and then they just got together in a room to talk about it once a week.

That would have been insane.

But they were eyewitnesses of God's majesty, so the only thing that made sense was to live lives that loved enemies and served orphans and widows and risked death to tell people about the Lord.

So, what have you seen and experienced? What are you a witness to?

Maybe you haven't seen people raised from the dead

or blind people healed, but I'm willing to bet you've experienced God in some very real ways in your life.

It doesn't take following Jesus for very long to start seeing Him show up in powerful ways.

But are we living like witnesses? Are we living in a way that makes sense based on what we've seen

17

LOCATION, LOCATION, LOCATION

When you enter a house, first say, "Peace to this house."

-Luke 10:5

I know a guy named Miles who's not the brightest person in the world. You know how a lot of times life just happens and bad things occur for reasons out of your control? Yeah, most of the bad things that have happened to Miles were because he's a bit of a moron.

Let me illustrate.

Miles had been looking for a job for months. He had been fired from his previous six jobs for reasons like lying on his application, not showing up, and eating the ingredients while he prepared hamburgers.

But he finally found someone willing to hire him, and it was actually a pretty good job.

Miles worked at the city jail and did the booking for new inmates. He would do their fingerprints and fill out their paperwork when they arrived.

It was probably the best job he'd ever had.

After working at the jail for a while, he started to get to know the prisoners. They were decent guys for the most part. Most of them were there for small crimes and just couldn't afford bail.

Miles mentioned to one of them that he lived out in the country, and the inmate told Miles that if he ever ran across some moonshine, let him know because he'd like to buy some.

As it turned out, Miles had a contact that lived just up the road from him that made his own moonshine.

Not wanting to miss out on an opportunity to make some extra money, the next day Miles got some moonshine from his neighbor and brought it to the jail to sell to that inmate.

However, when Miles informed the inmate that he had the moonshine, the inmate immediately told one of the jail's guards of the scheme, and Miles was promptly arrested.

And he also lost his job.

Who would have thought that it was a bad idea to try to sell homemade alcohol to a prisoner at a jail?

You see, Miles had forgotten one of the most basic facts of life: location, location, location.

Buying and selling moonshine on a farm outside of

town—not a big deal. Trying do it at the city jail—gets you arrested.

It's kind of like the difference between peeing in the pool and peeing *into* the pool.

Location is important.

And the same is true of serving others.

We have to know where we are.

One time I was in a lady's home in a third world country, and one of the people I was with said, "Wow, everything is so clean!"

That was a super offensive thing to say. Just because people live in poverty doesn't mean they don't take pride in their homes or value cleanliness. We have to be careful not to let our stereotypes fall out of our mouths.

I once served with a man who would wipe his feet off before approaching a homeless man's tent. He said it was what he did before entering his own home, so why should this be any different?

Exactly.

To be effective, we have to meet people where they are. We can't expect them to come to us.

But we have to be aware of what we say and do when we're on other people's home turf.

We can't assume we know what's best. We can't

assume we have all of the answers. We can't assume anything.

We have to get to know the people in our communities and find out what *they* think they need. We have to build relationships that honor who they are and where they're from.

There are so many different things involved. Race, gender, class, and history all make for extremely diverse communities. We have to be conscious of these things.

I'm not saying to walk around on eggshells and be hypersensitive or anything. I'm just saying let's be aware of our surroundings.

Let's not try to sell moonshine to inmates at the jail.

Let's realize that location is extremely important, and let's spend more time listening than talking. Let's learn about people and where they're from.

18

DRIVE BY JESUS

I no longer call you servants, because a servant does not know his master's business. Instead, I have called you friends, for everything that I learned from my Father I have made known to you.

-John 15:15

I'm a huge football fan. I spent a good number of years playing it, and I have a deep love for the game. So, Super Bowl Sunday is a big deal for me.

It's a little different now, but when I was younger, I made a full day out of it. I soaked up every once of coverage and stayed glued to the TV the entire day. I didn't want to miss a minute.

One Super Bowl Sunday, when I was in college, I came down to the dorm's lobby at 8AM. The dorm had a huge television surrounded by couches, so I came down to begin my fifteen-hour journey from pre-game predictions to post-game highlights.

I brought an illogical amount of food for one person and plopped myself down in front of the big screen.

About an hour into it, a girl came and sat down to my right on a different couch.

She was really pretty, but then she started to talk to me about football.

She became beautiful.

She asked me who I thought was going to win, and then we had a long conversation about the importance of defense in winning a game like this.

I remember thanking God for revealing the girl I was going to marry.

We talked for about thirty minutes, and it was a really great conversation.

There was a brief pause, and then she looked at me and smiled. Then she said something I'll never forget.

"So, do you know Jesus as your personal Lord and savior?"

I was confused. Where did that come from? What happened to talking about the finer details of a good halfback pass?

I said, "Yeah, I know Jesus."

To which she replied, "Okay, good."

This was a little perplexing, and I wasn't sure what to make of it. Then, about a minute later, she got up, said, "enjoy the game," and left.

And I never saw her again.

I had been had.

Everything about the last thirty minutes was a lie. The only reason she was talking to me was to get me saved. She didn't care about me or who I was or what my life was like. She wasn't interested in me in the slightest. (She probably didn't even like football.)

She just wanted to check a box.

I was furious. I had been nothing more than a project to her—just something potentially broken that she could fix—simply another line item on her agenda.

I felt used.

I felt played.

I had been a victim of drive by Jesus.

The Lord said to go make disciples—to make friends. He said to get to know people and build relationships.

However, that takes time. That's hard work. And that often requires a great deal of personal investment to do.

So, we tend to not want to do it. I mean, it's a whole lot easier not to. It's also a lot less uncomfortable if we just avoid the whole "make disciples" thing.

But notice what Jesus was really doing with the men He was leading. He was making friends. It wasn't this stilted, awkward thing. He was simply doing life with a group of guys that he really cared about.

And He was leading them to God.

I think a lot of times we look at Jesus' interactions with people in passing and we want to have the same results. Jesus was a pro at meeting people, knowing them for five minutes, and then completely changing their lives.

But let's not forget that Jesus is God.

In every single situation that Jesus changed someone's life through one conversation, He already knew everything about the person. He had the advantage of prior knowledge.

Jesus already knew Zacchaeus.

Jesus already knew the woman at the well.

Jesus already knew every single person He ever came into contact with, and not only did He know them, but He also had intimate knowledge of their past, present, and future.

We don't have that advantage.

We have to take the time to actually get to know people. We have to spend more than five minutes with them. We have to ask questions and listen.

Drive by Jesus only works for....Jesus.

That's why it's so important to get out in our

communities and befriend folks.

Real life change happens through relationships. It happens through shared experiences. It happens over time.

It doesn't happen through pretending to get to know someone and then sneak attacking him while he's trying to watch Super Bowl coverage.

I promise you that.

So, whether you're on a mission trip or at home, please get to know people. Learn their names. Learn their stories. Learn about what they're going through.

Build relationships.

Make friends.

And show them Jesus.

19

DOO-DOO BROWN
MICKEY MOUSE

Then God said, "Let us make mankind in our image, in our likeness, so that they may rule over the fish in the sea and the birds in the sky, over the livestock and all the wild animals, and over all the creatures that move along the ground."

So God created mankind in his own image, in the image of God he created them; male and female he created them.

-Genesis 1:26-27

A while back, my four-year-old daughter brought me a picture she had colored. It was a page out of a Disney coloring book with Mickey Mouse on it.

And my little girl, in her four-year-old wisdom, decided Mickey would look good if every part of his body was brown.

Deep.

Dark.

Doo-doo.

Brown.

Actually, most of the page was brown, and part of it was torn where she had ripped it out of the coloring book.

This was not exactly a piece of fine art. It didn't create the kind of moment when you think your child is destined for artistic greatness.

But, man, was she proud of that picture.

She came skipping over to me with this huge grin on her face, and she was so excited to show me the marvelous thing she had created.

Then, she handed it to me and said, "I made this for you."

And you know what I did?

I balled that garbage up and set it on fire. And then I sent her to her room for being proud of mediocre work.

No, of course that's not what I did.

That would be terrible. Only a complete monster would have that kind of reaction.

I love my daughter, so you know what I really did?

I told her how awesome she was and how much I appreciated my picture. Then I hung it on the refrigerator. I made a big deal about it. And doo-doo Mickey staid on the fridge for months.

That wasn't my reaction because the picture was any good. Even for a four-year-old, it was pretty bad art. But I love my little girl. I hung it up for all to see because of who created it not because of how it turned out.

How we treat the created shows how we feel about the creator.

The way we treat one another is the biggest indicator of how we feel about God.

Genesis tells us that God didn't just create us; He created us in His own image.

He didn't make a bunch of doo-doo brown Mickey Mouses. He made us in His likeness.

It can be hard to remember that sometimes. When loving and serving others, there are times when things just don't work out like we hope. There are times when people act like crap.

There have been times when I've been spit on and cussed out by people I was trying to help. There have been moments when I wanted to be absolutely done with people.

But God made them in the same likeness He created me in.

His.

And I know there are times when it would be a lot easier to just throw people away. But just like it would have been crazy to throw away my daughter's drawing, it would be even crazier to cast people aside.

So, as you go out and try to help people—as you try to serve the creation—remember this is really about the Creator and how we feel about Him.

20

THE SIDE OF ACTION

Do not merely listen to the word, and so deceive yourselves. Do what it says.

-James 1:22

My family eats dinner together every night. No phones. No TV. No arguing or complaining. We just sit down and enjoy a meal together.

When serving the food, I'll put meat and vegetables and bread on my daughter's plate in portion sizes I think she'll be able to eat. Then, I'll pour her some juice.

That little girl loves juice.

Then, I'll say, "Eat your food."

You know what I don't do?

I don't stand there looking over her shoulder telling her exactly how to eat.

I don't say, "Take two bites of your carrots. Now, eat some of your chicken. Let's go, let's go, let's go. Take one bite of bread. Take three sips of juice. Come on!"

That would be weird. I would be labeled a ridiculous control freak.

But I love my daughter, so there's no reason for me to treat her like that.

I just hand her a plate of food and tell her to enjoy it. If she wants to eat her chicken first, so be it. If she wants to drink all of her juice before eating any of her food, that's fine.

I just want her to eat and enjoy what has been provided for her.

Why do we so often act like God is any different?

Why do we sometimes get it in our heads that He's looking over our shoulders and barking orders about what we need to do with our lives?

And then we get nervous because maybe we misheard or maybe we haven't heard anything, and we don't want to screw things up.

But is this really how God, our loving Father, is? Is He really some weird control freak?

I don't think so.

I believe God has made it abundantly clear to us what He expects. We have a giant book of stories and commands straight from Him.

We know what He's looking for.

But then we'll sit around and wait for God to tell us what to do. We'll wait for some sign from heaven on exactly which path to take.

So many people take no action whatsoever because they're "waiting on the Lord." And while there's nothing wrong with being patient and waiting on doors to open or close, I meet a lot of people who are really just procrastinating and making excuses.

Ultimately, they're quite happy to live safe, comfortable, and boring lives while claiming they're "waiting on God to tell them what to do."

It sounds super spiritual, but more often than not, it's just an excuse to not do anything. And people will float through life for years "waiting on the Lord."

But what if God's plans aren't as specific as we think?

What if He just hands us a plate of food, says, "Eat and enjoy," and takes His seat at the table?

I think God has given each of us a plate full of talents, ideas, abilities, passions, and a host of other things, and He simply wants us to enjoy and use those things.

There are parameters of course, and we have to align what we do with what God expects, but maybe there's a good bit of leeway in how we live our lives.

For instance, if God has blessed you with a passion for photography, you can use that to go down lots of different roads. You could travel the world as a photojournalist. You could have a business and do school pictures. You could work for National Geographic and take pictures of wild animals. You could do lots of things with that.

Now, if you're going to follow Jesus, you obviously have to fit that passion for photography inside some certain stipulations. Working for Playboy and perpetuating lust and infidelity clearly wouldn't be what God had in mind when He blessed you with the ability to take great pictures.

We can't just do whatever we want and then ask God to bless it.

It would be no different than my daughter deciding to throw her food on the floor. There would be consequences, and she and I would have to talk through some things.

But is God really that concerned about whether you go to med school or law school? He's absolutely concerned about you as His child. But is He sitting on the edge of His seat hoping you'll make the right choice?

Maybe there's not a "right" choice in a lot of the things we get caught up on.

I meet so many people that are paralyzed by decisions. They don't want to make the wrong choice. They don't want to screw things up.

They want to make sure to follow "God's plan for their lives."

But here's the deal, **God does not have specific plans for most people's lives.**

Sure, He'll move things around and change things and put people and situations in your path, but most people do not have specific things that God has planned for them to do.

And if God has something specific He wants you to do, HE WILL TELL YOU SPECIFICALLY.

Throughout the entirety of human history, when God wants something done, He has been extraordinarily clear. There is no mistaking it.

So, unless burning bushes start talking to you or angels start appearing to you or you find yourself a virgin and pregnant, there's a really good chance that God's plan for your life isn't super specific.

We have to stop acting like "God's plan" is some mysterious, unknowable thing.

We have to stop treating the Bible like it's some giant riddle that we need a magical decoder ring to figure out what it says.

We have to stop sitting around waiting for a sign.

We've already had a sign from heaven. His name is Jesus.

And He made it overwhelmingly clear what God wants from His people.

I don't have to list all of the scriptures about loving

neighbors and enemies, feeding the hungry, visiting prisoners, taking care of widows and orphans, and helping the poor and downtrodden.

We know what the Bible says about taking care of the people in the world that God so loves.

Heck, Matthew 25 reads like a dang checklist for this stuff.

But then we have the audacity to pretend like we don't know what God wants from us?

So often we err on the side of caution, don't we. We don't want to mess up, so instead of trying to live out what God has commanded us, we'll do nothing.

It usually goes something like this: "God, I know that taking care of orphans is important to you, so I think maybe I should adopt a child. But I'm going to sit here and wait for you to tell me if that's what I should do." And then I wait and wait and wait.

But has God not already spoken?

I mean, how many scriptures talk about the importance of family? How many times does God talk about placing the fatherless and lonely into families?

What if instead of erring on the side of caution, we started erring on the side of action?

What would the world look like then?

What if situations went something like this: "God, I know that taking care of orphans is important to you, so I think maybe I should adopt a child. So, I'm going to start pursuing that, and if it's not what I should be doing right now, please let me know."

What if we started just doing what the Bible tells us to do, and if we start traveling down the wrong road, what if we started trusting that God would intervene?

What if we didn't wait for God to move us? What if we instead trusted God to stop us?

So, what does that look like?

Here's a simple formula:

1. What are you good at?

2. What needs do you see around you right now?

3. How do those two things intersect?

Let's go back to the photography example. Let's say you have a nice, little business doing wedding pictures. Then, you hear about some families living in a homeless shelter that can't afford to hire a photographer. So, you set up an event at the shelter to do family portraits for everyone there free of charge.

Your passion and ability just helped some people in need. It wasn't earth shattering, but changing the world usually isn't on the surface.

It's about doing little things to love and serve others using what God has blessed us with.

In Galatians, Paul tells us to do good to all people as

we have opportunity.

As we run into chances to help others, we don't have to consult God's plan for our lives. We know what to do, and we know what God expects from us.

He makes His plan for our lives really clear in three commands He gave us:

Love Him; love others; make disciples. (Luke 10:27, Matthew 28:19)

And that can manifest itself in a million different ways.

So, the question is how do the things God has blessed you with fit into those three commands?

How do your abilities show God you love Him? How does your passion love others? How do your talents help make disciples?

God's not breathing down our necks waiting to smack us because we ate our peas before our carrots.

He's not some control freak that gets angry if we wear red instead of blue.

And His plans aren't compromised based on any decisions that we make.

His plans go far beyond what school you decide to go to, what job you take, and who you marry. So, don't get so overwhelmed by not wanting to make the wrong decision that you fail to do anything.

And don't claim to be "waiting on the Lord" when

you're really just waiting for a decision to be made for you.

God is a loving father, and He's given us all plates full of opportunity. Let's enjoy them.

We know what He wants. Let's live like it.

Let's stop running from decisions and making excuses. Let's err on the side of action and go help a world that is waiting with breathless anticipation for the children of God to be revealed.

21

BETTER TO RECEIVE

In everything I did, I showed you that by this kind of hard work we must help the weak, remembering the words the Lord Jesus himself said: "It is more blessed to give than to receive."

-Acts 20:35

A few years ago, it was extremely cold outside, so my church opened up its gym to give the homeless a warm place to sleep.

I was asked to be in charge of the event, and I was pretty excited about it. The church had done this many times before, and I had been in charge of various aspects, but I had never run the entire thing.

This was no small task.

That night we brought in over 300 men, women, and children off the street, and there were over 100 volunteers involved doing everything from food prep in the fellowship hall to setting up beds in the gym. We also had lots of people there whose sole job was to sit down and talk to people and make sure they felt welcomed.

It was a lot to keep organized.

But I work for an awesome church with awesome people, and things were going smoothly.

Until they weren't.

We schedule things out so we never get overwhelmed in an area. And as long as we stick fairly close to the schedule, there are never any problems, no matter how many people we bring in.

But that night, some buses that had been dispatched to pick up people from various bridges and overpasses showed up late. And then some other buses showed up early.

This meant we had a huge influx of people at the same time. Instead of dealing with groups of twenty that were spaced out, we all of a sudden had a group of over a hundred coming in at the exact same moment.

Now, I'm not the kind of person that stresses out. I have a pretty calm demeanor no matter what. But I started to feel a little anxious when that many people came into the fellowship hall at the same time.

Having a lot of tired, cold, and hungry people in the same place can lead to problems.

Everyone formed a line for the food, and things seemed to be going well.

But then there was an argument among some people in line. A loud, colorful language filled argument. Apparently, someone was trying to cut in line, and the people behind him didn't appreciate it.

It was just words and insults at first, but that led to a push, and that led to a fight. Now, it wasn't a stereotypical fight with fists being thrown. It was more of an awkward hugging match. Both men were wearing big, heavy coats, which made it hard to move around and definitely made it hard to fight.

A couple security guards broke up the fight and escorted the men out of the fellowship hall.

About that time, another busload of people arrived.

I'm not gonna lie, at this point, I started to stress out a little bit.

I really needed to move some of these people to the gym. It was important to lower the number of people that were cooped up around each other.

But at the same time, I didn't want to send a big group of people to the gym if they weren't ready to receive them. I didn't want to overwhelm them while they were still trying to set up beds. They had been working for a while, but 300+ air mattresses with sheets, blankets, and pillows take time.

Another argument broke out. Someone allegedly touched someone else's butt, and now the whole room was hearing about it.

I took my phone out and called the lady in charge of the gym setup.

She didn't pick up.

I called her again.

She picked up, but the gym has bad reception, so it was hard for me to hear her. It was a conversation with a lot of "What?" and "Can you repeat that?"

I finally heard enough to understand that the gym wasn't ready yet.

Great.

I was trying to figure out how much more time they needed, but she couldn't hear me. I asked a few times, but no response.

Then, she hung up.

I was more than frustrated by this point.

I said, "Dang it!" and slammed my phone down on the table in front of me.

The men in the food line in front of me took a quick step back. My outburst had caught them a little off-guard.

I stood there for a moment trying to regain composure.

After a few seconds, I smiled and apologized to the men for startling them. I thanked them for joining us and wished them a good evening.

I had pulled myself together on the outside, but the inside was still frustrated and annoyed.

One of the men in line looked at me and smiled.

I asked him what his name was and he replied, "Terrance."

I said, "Terrance, do you know Jesus?"

He said, "Man, I love Jesus!"

I replied, "Then, would you mind praying for me? I'm a little stressed out right now."

You would have thought I had asked Terrance if he wanted a hundred dollars. He said, "Absolutely!" and walked over and put his hand on my shoulder.

Then, he prayed a short prayer asking for peace and for God to remove my stress.

And it was exactly what I needed.

As he prayed for me, my stress level diminished. My frustration and annoyance went away. And I felt peace wash over me.

Everything was going to be all right.

There were over 300 people that were being fed and loved on, and they were going to have a warm place to sleep.

That was the important thing. The schedule would work itself out.

When we serve, it's so easy put ourselves in the power position.

We're here to give; you're here to receive. But this isn't how it's supposed to work.

One-way giving is never the best way to do things.

And **you will never minister effectively to anyone you think less of.**

To truly love and serve others, we have to allow them to love and serve as well. We have to be willing to share our own shortcomings and needs and allow them to minister to us.

On that night, I was serving Terrance, and it would have been easy to pretend like I was the have and he was the have-not. But that would have been a lie.

We were both have-nots.

He didn't have a warm place to sleep, and I didn't have peace.

But in serving each other, we both ended up having what we needed.

So, when you're out serving, please remember that it's awesome and blessed to give, but there are also times when it's better to receive.

22

WHEN THE ARMOR DOESN'T FIT

Then Saul dressed David in his own tunic. He put a coat of armor on him and bronze helmet on his head. David fastened his own sword over the tunic and tried walking around, because he was not used to them.

"I cannot go in these," he said to Saul, "because I am not used to them." So he took them off. Then he took his staff in his hand, chose five smooth stones from the stream, put them in the pouch of his shepherd's bag and, with his sling in his hand, approached the Philistine.

-1ˢ Samuel 17:38-40

A few years ago, I was introduced to a guy named Greg after a church service. We had a short conversation, and I could tell that something big was happening in his life. He seemed to have this interesting excitement in his voice. I thought he had just gotten engaged or something.

I asked him what was going on in his life. And he said,

"I'm leaving for Uganda tomorrow."

"Oh, that's really cool," I replied. "What are you going to do there?"

"I don't know yet," he said. "God just told me to go, so I'm going."

"For how long?" I asked.

Greg smiled. "I'm not sure. I just got a one-way ticket."

I was a little perplexed. "So, you're going to Uganda for an undetermined amount of time and not sure what you're going to do..."

"Yeah," Greg said excitedly like there was nothing strange about that.

"And what about your life here?" I asked.

"Well, I dropped out of college and sold all my stuff," he said. "So there's nothing keeping me tied down here."

"What about your parents?" I asked.

"They're not too excited about it, but it'll be alright," he said. "God said go, so I have to go."

Now, you might be sitting there thinking that Greg was out of his mind. It's crazy to drop everything and head off into the unknown like that.

But let me remind you that there were twelve young men who did the same thing about 2,000 years ago, and that changed the entire world.

No, Greg wasn't crazy, he just realized that his armor didn't fit.

Throughout his life, he had been told the same things society tells all of us. Go to college. Get a job. Get married. Have 2.5 kids. Get a dog and a mortgage. Invest in your 401k. And so on.

And while there's nothing wrong with these things— these are all good things—it wasn't the kind of life that fit Greg.

What society was telling him to do wasn't lining up with what God was telling him to do. And unlike many Christians, he broke from society and went down the path God was setting before him.

What was so interesting about Greg is that there wasn't an ounce of fear in his voice. He was about to embark on an unknown adventure, and he didn't know what to expect or when he would come back. Yet, he didn't appear to be afraid at all.

He didn't know what was next, but he knew who was in control.

When David was about to fight Goliath, it made a lot of sense to put some armor on. To go to war against a giant would require a breastplate and a helmet. It would require a sword.

But when David put it on, it didn't fit right. The armor actually made it harder for him to fight.

But instead of thinking, "Well, it doesn't fit, but people

are telling me I need it, so I'll keep wearing it," he took the armor off.

Can you imagine the courage it took to remove that armor and go grab some rocks for a slingshot?

Everyone on the battlefield thought he was either out of his mind or an idiot.

But David just knew what he had been called to do. And more importantly, he knew who had called him to do it.

We all run into situations in life when people try to tell us what our lives should look like. And this advice can often be really good. People who love us and want what's best for us will often lead us in the right direction.

But there are times when the expectations from others don't line up with how God is leading.

There are times when we have to decide the armor doesn't fit.

The church is notorious for trying to put out people's fires. No one would ever admit that's what's happening, but as soon as you start trying to do something unexpected, people will come out of nowhere to tell you it's a bad idea.

Can you imagine the opposition Greg got from fellow Christians?

I bet tons of people made it a point to tell him to "pray more about that decision." I'm sure he heard "Are you really sure God is calling you to that?" more than once. Or "You'll regret dropping out of school when you're older."

I've seen people in the church squelch a person's fire far more times than people who don't know Jesus.

Now, I'm not saying that to criticize the church. I just want you to be ready for the pushback. If you're reading this book, it means there's a good chance that God is calling you to something different. It's not better or worse than what He's called other people to. It's just different.

Maybe you've been walking around for a while in armor that you know doesn't fit.

Maybe you've felt God leading you in a direction you know you should go in, but you're nervous about what others will think.

I get it.

But this is your life.

So, I want to encourage you to do what God is calling you to do. It may be scary. It might require you to give up some things. It could put you on an unknown path.

But if you know for a fact that God is at the center of it, you have to go that way.

If God is for you, who can be against you?

After that brief conversation with Greg, I never saw him again. As far as I know, he got on a plane to

Uganda the next day. And you know what, I bet he had an incredible adventure.

I can't wait to run into Greg again, either in this life or the next, and hear the stories he has to tell because there's not a doubt in my mind that God showed up in some powerful ways.

That's the thing about God. Incredible things happen when we go where He's leading.

23

PERSISTENCE

Therefore, my dear brothers and sisters, stand firm. Let nothing move you. Always give yourselves fully to the work of the Lord, because you know that your labor in the Lord is not in vain.

-1st Corinthians 15:58

In college, the football team I played for had an absolutely incredible strength coach. He was a hard man, but he knew exactly how to get the best out of us. He also had a tendency to say things that would really put life into perspective.

One time, during summer workouts, a bunch of guys on the team were complaining about how hard the workouts were and how sore their legs were. They were making all sorts of excuses as to why they weren't doing well.

After one workout, the strength coach gathered us up around him and said something I will never forget.

"Men, I know a lot of you are having a tough time right now. I realize you're dealing with some pretty serious soreness. But I want you to know there's three things you can do for that: **Eat, hydrate, and get over it.**"

And while this wasn't the answer that a lot of us wanted to hear, it was definitely what needed to be said. Things weren't going to get any easier, so we might as well just get over it.

As Christians, we often need to follow the same advice. When it's hard to live out the Bible, when it's easy to make excuses, and when it's tough to love God and love people, we need to just eat, hydrate, and get over it.

We keep going because we know how the story ends. The Bible is quite clear on how it all turns out.

We're not sitting on the sidelines watching Jesus fight against the world and hoping He comes out on top. He's already overcome the world.

He already won.

That means nothing we do for Him and His glory will ever be in vain.

There are times when we work and pray and believe and hope, and nothing turns out the way we want. But we can rest assured that every tear and drop of sweat shed for the Kingdom's sake is well-spent effort.

Things might take longer to come to fruition, or we

might not even be the ones to see the fruit, but we can continue to work in confidence knowing that God is in control.

In man's world, hard work doesn't always pay off. We like to think it does, but there are plenty of hard-working people who never realized their dreams. There are plenty of talented folks who did everything they could to accomplish something but fell short.

That's life.

But in God's world, hard work always pays off. The effort always leads to something that matters.

That's because God's world is all about people. They are what is most important. So, everything we do to love, serve, and help others matters.

We just have to keep fighting the good fight.

We have to say persistent.

Do you remember the story about Jacob wrestling with God in Genesis 32?

What appears to be a man grabs hold of Jacob and wrestles with him throughout an entire night. When the man realizes he can't overpower Jacob, he injures Jacob's hip and demands to be let go.

But Jacob replies, "I will not let go unless you bless me."

And the man, who turns out to be God, blesses Jacob and gives him the new name of Israel.

Persistence.

Not letting go.

Continuing to fight and hold on no matter what.

That's what the people of the world need from the followers of Jesus.

I know it's easier to walk away. I realize it's easier to just give up. But we have to continue to stand firm. We have to continue to love God and love others.

We have to continue to give ourselves fully to the work of the Lord knowing that the labor and energy and sweat and tears and everything else that goes with it will not be in vain.

No matter what comes along to deter us, we have to eat, hydrate, and get over it.

24

A DIFFERENT KIND

But Zacchaeus stood up and said to the Lord, "Look, Lord! Here and now I give half of my possessions to the poor, and if I have cheated anybody out of anything, I will pay back four times the amount."

-Luke 19:8

If you couldn't tell, I absolutely love the story of Zacchaeus.

I love how he stopped at nothing to see Jesus. I love how there was an obstacle in his way, and he literally climbed over it to be able to see the Lord.

I love how we get to see another instance of Jesus loving someone no one else cared for. And as a crooked tax collector, people were definitely not fond of Zacchaeus.

But most importantly, I love how Zacchaeus allowed Jesus to totally transform his life but *didn't* sell everything and become the 13th disciple.

So often, it's easy to fall into the trap of thinking there are different levels of Christ followers.

It's easy to think that people who sell everything to go live in a third world country to be missionaries are somehow on a higher level than a soccer mom who stays at home and raises four kids.

Or we think that the drug addict who came to know Jesus in prison and now helps get homeless people off the street is somehow a better follower of Jesus than a janitor that cleans the same hallways for thirty years.

The story of Zacchaeus shows us that it's not about doing what Christian culture tells us are grand, wonderful things.

No, ultimately, it's about being a different kind of whatever God has placed it in your heart to be.

Zacchaeus didn't sell everything, give the proceeds to the poor, and fall in line with the rest of the disciples.

That's not what Jesus called him to do.

Instead, Zacchaeus became a different kind of tax collector.

He paid back anyone he had ever swindled and became honest in his work.

And that's what the world needs more of.

More Christians heeding the call to be missionaries would be amazing.

But more Christians heeding the call to be different kinds of doctors, lawyers, janitors, teachers, and etc. would be world changing.

Most people aren't called to sell everything and become missionaries. However, anyone who follows Jesus is called to be different.

It's time to get over the idea of there being different levels of Christians, and it's time to stop buying the lie that ministry should be left up to the "professionals" (i.e. pastors, missionaries, youth directors).

It's time to realize that Jesus has called all of us to different things—different places, different professions, different lifestyles, etc.

But He has called us all to live in a way that reflects Him and loves others.

He's called us to be a different kind.

25

SUPPLY

As Jesus stepped ashore, He saw a huge crowd, felt compassion for them, and healed their sick. When evening came, the disciples approached Him and said, "This place is a wilderness, and it is already late. Send the crowds away so they can go into the villages and buy food for themselves."

"They don't need to go away," Jesus told them. "You give them something to eat."

"But we only have five loaves and two fish here," they said to Him.

"Bring them here to Me," He said. Then He commanded the crowds to sit down on the grass. He took the five loaves and the two fish, and looking up to heaven, He blessed them. He broke the loaves and gave them to the disciples, and the disciples gave them to the crowds. Everyone ate and was filled. Then they picked up 12 baskets full of leftover pieces! Now those who ate were about 5,000 men, besides women and children.

-Matthew 14:14-21

I have a friend who loves Chic-Fil-A. I mean he looooves it. He could eat there three times a day and not get tired of it. And one cool thing about Chick-Fil-A is that every time they open a new restaurant, they give a year's supply of meals to the first 100 people in the store.

My friend has been one of the first 100 on three separate occasions. He's slept outside in the cold just to be the first in line before. Like I said, the dude loves the place.

But here's the deal with that "year's supply" of food: it's really just 52 coupons for free meals. They assume a rational person is only going to eat there once a week, so 52 coupons would last a year.

However, my friend is no rational person when it comes to the home of the chicken sandwich (and to be fair, neither am I, that stuff is delicious.) So, all three of his "year's supplies" only ever lasted around three months. That's right. He used up 52 free meals in less than 90 days.

And I got to thinking, this is pretty typical when it comes to man's supply. It's supposed to last a certain amount of time, but it never does.

I've got deodorant that claims "72 hour protection." That's a joke. Maybe if I don't move around or ever put my arms down.

My wife has "long lasting" makeup. But it seems she and the makeup have different ideas about what a long time really is.

All around us, things are constantly making bold claims. And all around us things are letting us down.

That's why the feeding of the 5000 is one of my favorite stories in all of scripture. I love it for what it teaches us about supply and demand.

Just look at the difference in how the disciples approach the situation compared to how Jesus handles it.

The disciples look at the crowd. It's huge. Then, they look at their watches. It's late. Then, they look around for a place for all of those people to eat. It's not there.

So, they get together and make a rational and wise decision. The people should be sent home. It's been real. It's been fun. Some parts have even been real fun, but there's no food here, so it's time to call it a day.

They feel good about the decision. It makes sense. So, they go to Jesus to let Him know the plan.

And then Jesus says something ridiculous. "Don't send them away. Feed them."

The disciples get a little sarcastic. "You want us to feed over 5000 people with just three fish sandwiches? Quit playing, Jesus."

It's easy to judge the disciples for not having faith in this moment, but let's be honest, we would have been right there with them.

They were doing exactly what we do so often: focusing on the demand.

They were looking at a huge group of people and comparing it to a tiny basket of food. The demand was too great. It would be impossible to feed that many people with so little.

And that's just like us on pretty much a daily basis.

We wake up in the morning and immediately start focusing on the demands of the day. Meetings. Presentations. Tests. Bosses. Clients. Teachers. Coaches. We think through what's going to be required of us, and we usually wish we had done a little more the day before to prepare.

Then, we get a little stressed. A little anxious. A little worried. What if I can't meet the demands? What if I fail? What if I'm not good enough?

We play out scenario after scenario of how things could go. We go through conversations in our heads. We make points and counterpoints to people in our imagination. We waste a lot of time on things that will never happen the way we think.

But look at Jesus in this story.

He tells the disciples to bring him the food. Then, He tells the demand to sit down.

And then, He looks up to heaven.

He looks to the supply.

Jesus is fully aware of the demand that is before Him. He's not oblivious to how many people are there.

He just knows the supply is greater.

Not only did all 5000+ people get fed that day, they also picked up twelve baskets of leftovers! And that's the difference between man's supply and God's supply.

Every morning, God supplies us with enough of what we need for that day. As we roll out of bed, He's already provided enough grace, strength, mercy, peace, and everything else for that day.

He knows the day's demands. He knows what we're going to need to make it through. And He supplies us with enough to do so.

We're told to ask God to give us our "daily bread." Not weekly or monthly or yearly bread, but our daily bread. Because that's how God's supply works. That's where the trust comes in.

For the Israelites in the wilderness, the Manna fell from heaven each morning. And whether the people gathered a lot or a little, they had just enough for that day.

The same is true for us. **Each morning, the Manna falls.**

Life is hard. Serving others is hard. The demands are high every single day.

But just know that every day, God has already given you what you need. The supply is already there.

AFTERWORD

When I was in high school, I went on tons of mission trips. And every time, I would have this really cool spiritual high when I got back. I would have this awesome fire going. Things would be different.

But it would always fade.

It wouldn't be long before I was back to normal, and my trip was a fond memory and something nice to look back on, but nothing more.

Life would happen, and I'd find myself right back in the same habits and routines that I had before.

It was almost like there was a switch that I'd turn on for the mission trip, and when I got back home, I'd turn the switch back off.

The fire always burnt out.

There were times when I felt really disappointed in myself for not keeping the fire going. I didn't understand how the fire could burn so brightly when I was off serving others and then disappear when I got back home.

Years later, I realized what I was doing wrong. I finally figured out what the problem was.

Perspective.

On a mission trip, I would experience a giant, raging bonfire. That's common. It's normal. You've probably experienced something similar.

But when I got back home, I would stop feeding the fire.

I got into an all or nothing mentality. I either had to be totally wrapped up in mission work 24/7 or not at all.

But that's the wrong way to look at things.

That's not sustainable.

Anyone who's ever been camping will tell you that keeping a fire going doesn't mean you put all of your firewood on at the same time.

That'll burn big and bright for a little while, but it's not going to last. It won't be long until the whole thing is nothing but ash.

No, to keep a fire going, you feed it a little at the time.

And likewise, keeping your fire going after a mission trip works the same way.

It's not about going home, starting a bunch of programs and non-profits, and saving the world.

It's about seeing the opportunities to serve that are constantly crossing your path and taking the time and making the effort to love the people right there in front of you.

It's about carrying your cross daily and walking in the direction God is leading.

Daily.

You want to change the world?

Do it one day at a time. One moment at a time.

Wash the dishes.

Get to know the people who live across the street.

Stop being so busy all the time.

You want to keep the fire going?

Feed it one log at a time.

And, sure, starting a non-profit or really cool program to help people may be part of that. But grand gestures aren't sustainable.

Keeping the fire going requires little things done with great love.

So, get out there.

Go change someone's day.

ABOUT THE AUTHOR

Gabe spends the majority of the year living and serving in Honduras with his awesome wife and beautiful little girls. He's also the founder and director of the M25 Mission Camp and, during the summer, leads mission trips in Atlanta, GA that connect high school and college students with people on the street experiencing homelessness.

For more from Gabe, check out BetterMissions.com where he is the founder and editor of a blog on serving people with excellence.

57238742R00095

Made in the USA
Lexington, KY
09 November 2016